Local Business Goldmine

Goldmine's Essential Guide

[O. Addey]

Copyright © 2021 *O. Addey*

All rights reserved.

Table of Contents

Introduction 6
Chapter-01: Turn your Local Business goldmine 7
    An innovative business idea 7
    The right talent 8
    Your network 9
    Hard work 9
    Sales 10
Chapter-02: How to begin a genuine fresh start? ... 12
    Genuine need 13
    Credible experience 13
    Adequate Resources 14
    Buying Customers 14
    Sound Business Model 15
Chapter-03: How to Grow A Successful Business 17
    Get Organized 17
    Keep Detailed Records 17
    Analyze Your Competition 18
    Understand the Risks and Rewards 18
    Be Creative 18
    Stay Focused 19
    Prepare to Make Sacrifices 19

Provide Great Service 19

Be Consistent 19

Chapter-04: How to proceed from the very first 20

Provide a Great Product or Service 20

Do Your Research 21

Keep Things Organized 22

Detailed Record Keeping 23

Keep Focus & Have Patience 24

Be Prepared to Make Difficult Decisions 25

Keep Your Overhead to a Minimum 26

Know the Operational Needs 26

Hire the Right People and Treat Them Well 27

Always Look to Improve 28

Chapter-05: How to Make Your Small Business More Successful 30

Focus on Customer Service 30

Build Word of Mouth for Your Business 30

Expand Your Marketing Efforts 31

Build Your Online Presence 32

Testimonials from customers 32

Cut Your Business Costs 32

Go Mobile 33

Get in the Cloud 33
Find and Keep the Right Employees 34
Update Your Business Plan 34
Stay Balanced 35
Make This Your Best Year Ever 35
Conclusion 37

Introduction

To thrive in business today, you must be adaptable and have strong planning and organizing abilities. Many people start a business with the expectation that they would switch on their computers or open their doors and start generating money, only to discover that making money in a business is far more difficult than they anticipated. Do you feel like you're treading water in your small business and not making any forward toward your objectives? Or are you having difficulties deciding which business goals to pursue this year in the first place? Of course, every entrepreneur desires to run a successful and lucrative firm, but it is not always apparent how to do it. If you want your small business to be more lucrative than ever before, here are some ideas to help you get there. And keep in mind that running a successful business is a marathon, not a sprint. You may avoid this in your business efforts by taking your time and laying out all the procedures essential for success. Whatever sort of business you wish to establish, adopting the nine tips below can help you be successful.

Chapter-01: Turn your Local Business goldmine

People are drawn to owning a business for a variety of reasons. You get to be your boss, work with incredible people, set your hours, and convert a hobby into a profession. However, it is not without difficulty. Often, first-time entrepreneurs dive in headfirst and are caught off guard by the realities of running a business. So, what does it take to start a profitable business? Through a HARO inquiry, I chatted with numerous company owners and identified five significant drivers to business success.

An innovative business idea

If you want to have a chance of surviving, especially in a competitive sector, you must figure out what distinguishes you from the other alternatives. Clever marketing or fascinating technology alone will not ensure that your target clients are stunned by what you're giving; you must also provide actual value and a novel experience.

Richard Werbe, the creator of the micro-tutoring platform StudyPool, describes his method for developing a unique company concept, adding, "You must be aware of current trends. Most individuals believe that they must come up with an original concept. Still, you may use current popular trends and expand on what you're currently seeing out there to create a better service or product."

Nothing else will determine whether your firm will succeed or fail; having an original product or service that will be well-received is one method to stack the odds in your favor. You don't have to recreate anything fully; only improve it.

The right talent

Long-term company success necessitates assembling the appropriate personnel to create your brand. Your staff is the backbone of your firm, and one malignant employee may utterly derail your development. Whether you're assembling an on-site team or a remote workforce, one thing stays constant: the appropriate people coupled with the same goal can dramatically increase your chances of success. Top-Notch Threads creator Kip Skibicki knows the value of creating an all-star staff. "When I began my firm, I didn't have a lot of contacts, but I was devoted to developing a team that shared my vision and had the necessary expertise and know-how for each job," Skibicki said. During the initial period, building a business takes a significant lot of effort. However, long hours and the up-and-down roller coaster ride are far more fun when the entire team is eager to work together to achieve objectives and milestones.

Your network

Creating a personal network of like-minded entrepreneurs provides several advantages. First, it provides a sounding board for when you have questions or need guidance, which is quite beneficial, especially in the early phases of a firm. Second, as your network expands, so will your resources.

I'm a member of numerous professional organizations and am often networking. Personally, my network has been a major part of my success, and witnessing how valuable it has been inspired me to launch the Mastermind House, a unique virtual networking option for entrepreneurs. "A robust network may assist any organization, from a major legal firm to a small single-member startup. As you develop trust in networking, your network's size and capability to help you solve problems and make smart business decisions grows. I strongly encourage you to make time in your calendar for networking, "Adam Zayed, founding partner of Zayed Law Offices, says.

Hard work

You might as well not start if you're not willing to get your hands filthy and work in the trenches. Unfortunately, many would-be entrepreneurs have a distorted view of what it's like to run a firm. The startup life is romanticized in the media, but it isn't all Lamborghinis and private aircraft. If you want to be successful, you must be willing to put in the effort.

Zac Grove worked as a consultant for several educational technology businesses before founding the American International English Teachers' Association. This allowed him to understand the ins and outs of the industry, which he eventually applied to his passion project.

"After working in ed-tech, I recognized that my life's passion was launching solutions to effect change. I would never have had the courage to go out on my own if I hadn't first paid my dues and learned the ins - outs of running a successful business while working for someone else, "Grove explains. Consider gaining the necessary abilities, insights, and experience by working for another firm; it's a feasible alternative that can pay off in the long run.

Sales

One factor that can quickly indicate the viability of your product or service is sales. Sales not only indicate that you have a viable product, but they also bring money into your company, allowing you to grow and avoid failure.

Carlo Cisco is the creator and CEO of Select, a private community that provides members with access to special events and discounts at restaurants, hotels, nightclubs, and stores. Cisco stressed sales from the start to establish a presence for his company.

"As an entrepreneur, you're always selling your vision to existing and potential workers, partners, investors, and advisers," Cisco adds. "Know your pitch and practice it constantly. You must be comfortable pitching one-on-one, in front of a group of hundreds, or to senior executives."

Ideas are fantastic, but without sales to back them up, they are doomed to fail. Mark Cuban is always emphasizing the importance of sales in determining success. Entrepreneurs that excel in sales provide their companies with a competitive advantage.

Chapter-02: How to begin a genuine fresh start?

I've seen a lot of entrepreneurs thrive, and a lot of them fail over the years. Those that are successful often have five components in place before beginning their company. First, there must be a demonstrable need for the product (NEED). Second, you must have the necessary skills and reputation to begin your business (EXPERIENCE). Third, you must have all the necessary resources to get started, including personnel, production, distribution, and finances (RESOURCES). Fourth, you must have consumers who are dedicated to purchasing your goods (CUSTOMERS). Finally, your company strategy must be robust, from pricing and cost of goods through gross margin and profit margin (MODEL).

The stronger these five elements are, the more likely you are to succeed. On the other hand, the fewer these elements there are, the greater your chances of failing. So let's go through these five elements of a genuine opportunity in further depth.

Genuine need

True business possibilities satisfy people's demands or alleviate their pain spots. Being deeply involved in a certain sector or business is the greatest method to uncover these requirements and pain spots. Most successful entrepreneurs have worked in the industry where they start their firm in a similar field or had personal familiarity with the goods, services, and issues. They identify a need and validate it via direct observation. Joining a think tank, learning to brainstorm, or sitting in a university lecture usually does not lead to discovering pressing needs.

I can't tell you how many wannabe entrepreneurs I've met have fallen in love with a concept because it's brilliant, cute, and even entertaining. The only difficulty is that no one requires, desires, or is ready to pay for it. "You have a fantastic solution—now discover a problem it solves," I urge them. But, of course, it's considerably easier to do it the other way around: first, identify the problem, then devise a remedy. If you require the goods for personal reasons, that is fantastic. If all of your friends, family members, coworkers, and business associates require it, that's even better.

Credible experience

Knowing about an industry's goods, services, and challenges not only helps you avoid the pitfalls of trial-and-error learning but also offers interested parties confidence that you're the ideal person to develop this firm. Potential team members, investors, consumers, suppliers, and strategic partners value your experience and reputation. You'll be fighting an uphill battle if you don't have the abilities and expertise to develop your firm. It is essential to seek out advisers, partners, and team members who can cover holes in your skillset when this occurs. Finally, you and your team will need the required expertise and reputation to grow your firm.

Adequate Resources

Many would-be entrepreneurs believe they need money to launch their new firm; there is no business without money. In reality, successful entrepreneurs use various resources to get started, including working from home, finding mentors and advisors, using free software, acquiring used equipment, bartering and trading, partnering with their first customers, obtaining credit from suppliers, and borrowing before renting or buying. The essential thing is to figure out what your new enterprise will require, then go out and locate the tools you'll need to get started. You may not necessarily require funds, but you do require resources.

Buying Customers

As soon as they begin their enterprises, smart entrepreneurs have consumers committed to purchasing their products or services. Dave Twombly, for example, had clients waiting for him to establish his waste firm. Patrick Hayden's weapons and accessories were already in high demand. And, before establishing her marketing firm, Joanne McCall sold her first contract to her employer. When you have particular consumers eager to purchase your product as soon as you open your company, you have ultimate confirmation of your solution, quick revenues, and early cash flow from which to expand. Selling your items or services before you debut is usually a good idea. If you can't accomplish it, you might not be ready.

Sound Business Model

Your business model determines how you will generate money in your enterprise. It contains your revenue sources, pricing, costs of products sold, gross margin, operational costs, and profit margin – in other words, the parts of an income statement. It provides solutions to the following questions:

- What are the various client groups I serve? (sources of revenue)
- What will they pay for my goods? (revenue) How much would it cost me to manufacture these products? How much do I profit from each sale? (cost of products) (profit margin)
- What are the operating costs for my business? (Operating expenses)
- How much money does the company make after all expenses? (profitability)

The greatest firms have diverse revenue streams, competitive pricing, a gross margin of 50% or more, and a 10% to 20% profit margin. It will be tough to survive if your stats aren't as appealing. So, before you start your business, make sure all of the figures add up.

The failure rate for new enterprises is quite high: 50% fail after five years, and 70% fail within 10. This, I believe, is because individuals launch ideas rather than opportunities. When you launch a concept, you use up all of your resources before you can sort things out, get traction, and make money.

Chapter-03: How to Grow A Successful Business

Starting a business necessitates analytical thinking, focused organization, and meticulous recordkeeping. It is critical to be aware of your competition and either emulate or improve on their successful strategies. You'll almost definitely wind up working harder for yourself than you would for someone else, so be prepared to make personal sacrifices while starting your firm. Finally, it is critical to provide excellent service to your consumers to win their loyalty and maintain their business.

Get Organized

You must be organized to attain business success. It will assist you in completing chores and staying on top of things to accomplish. Creating a to-do list each day is a wonderful approach to stay organized. Check each thing off your list as you finish it. This will guarantee that you don't forget anything and that you do all of the critical duties to the sustainability of your organization.

Keep Detailed Records

Every successful firm keeps meticulous records. This way, you'll know where your company is financially and what potential problems you could face. Knowing this provides you time to devise methods to overcome such obstacles.

Analyze Your Competition

The best outcomes are produced via competition. Therefore, you must not be scared to study and learn from your rivals if you want to succeed. After all, they may be doing something profitable that you can replicate in your firm.

Understand the Risks and Rewards

Taking measured risks to help your business development is the key to success. A smart question to ask is, "What's the disadvantage?" If you can answer this question, you are aware of the worst-case situation. This information will enable you to take measured risks that can yield enormous benefits. Understanding risks and benefits entail making sound decisions about when to launch your firm. For example, did the severe economic dislocation of 2020 present you with an opportunity (for example, producing and selling face masks) or a hindrance (for example, launching a new restaurant at a period of social distance and restricted seating allowed)?

Be Creative

Always be on the lookout for ways to improve your business and differentiate it from the competition. Recognize that you don't know everything and have an open mind to fresh ideas and methods for your business.

Stay Focused

The ancient adage "Rome wasn't built in a day" fits here. Just because you start a business does not imply you will start generating money right away. It takes time to let others know who you are, so focus on completing your short-term objectives.

Prepare to Make Sacrifices

The road to beginning a business is difficult, but once you open your doors, your job has only just begun. You may need to put in more time than you would if you were working for someone else to be successful, which may mean spending less time with family and friends.

Provide Great Service

Many successful firms overlook the need to deliver excellent customer service. If you give superior service to your clients, they will be more likely to return to you instead of turning to your rival the next time they need anything.

Be Consistent

Consistency is essential for generating money in business. Therefore, you must continue to do what is required to be successful daily. This will help you develop long-term beneficial habits that will assist you in making money in the long run.

Chapter-04: How to proceed from the very first

Every entrepreneur desires to build a successful and lucrative firm; this is a simple and self-evident statement. However, most small company entrepreneurs can not transform their idea into a small business success. According to the Bureau of Labor Statistics, 65 percent of new firms in the United States fail within the first five years, with just 25 percent lasting 15 years or more (U.S. Bureau of Labor Statistics, 2019.) So, how can an entrepreneur break into a small company's success rate? Let's go through how you may enter your firm into the Hall of Fame for Small Business Success Stories.

Provide a Great Product or Service

While marketing is important for building awareness and bringing visitors to your brand, it can only go you so far. Once the consumers arrive, the items or services must be good enough to meet or exceed their expectations. This is how you develop a life-long repeat consumer who will support the business by spreading the news. Making consumers become brand ambassadors is one of the most successful and cost-effective methods to get a small business noticed. However, this can only happen if the product is of high quality and, most all, delivers an excellent solution to a real problem that satisfies market demand. Unfortunately, many entrepreneurs have created mind-blowing and creative goods that fail, while others with a simple idea dominate the market — Why? Perhaps the first group became so focused on the final product that they simply neglected to address an issue. In contrast, the second group discovered a common problem to which many potential consumers can connect.

Do Your Research

Business is never simply business; it must be extremely personal as well. However, this does not mean that entrepreneurs should throw caution to the wind and launch enterprises based entirely on their preferences. For example, you may believe that walking a cat on a leash is a fantastic idea, but will a cat leash business be successful? Gut instincts are useful, but they are not the same as information. It is derived from data, which is derived through study. What is the size of the prospective consumer base, and what qualities do these people have? To effectively target consumer profiles, it is important to understand what drives and motivates them. One of the most important elements to small company success is research.

Sonsoles Gonzalez's Better Not Younger is a small company success story. A 54-year-old beauty industry veteran with over 30 years of combined experience at the giants Procter & Gamble and L'Oréal spotted a market gap for a hair care specialist brand intended for older women. In addition, she noticed that all of the main hair care manufacturers' target clients were women aged 18 to 44. As a result, Better Not Younger opted to target its communication efforts on stylish and smart women. "Women over the age of 50 control $20 trillion in net wealth. They spend 2.5 times as much as the typical customer. They're active on social media.

The competitive assessment is another important component of research. To develop a brand that meets the market's demands, you must first comprehend the playing field. So here are a few questions you should think about asking: Is there any firm that might be considered a competitor? What can you learn from your rivals? Is there one that jumps out as a leader in the industry? If that's the case, how did they get to number one? What were the secrets to their small company's success? Have they made any errors that you might have avoided?

Finding out that your small firm has no potential competitors may be both a gift and a warning sign. Is there a reason for their absence? What can you learn from what drove them out of business if they did exist? The study will maintain the emphasis on a small firm honest. If you want to be a part of the small company success tales, you must not alter the information to match your gut instincts.

Keep Things Organized

This point cannot be overstated. Access to information quickly and effectively will make a huge impact in the everyday operations of a small business, whether it is through a real file cabinet or an ordered digital folder structure in your computer. It is strongly advised to have distinct folders for each business area that are correctly labeled and structured to make sense to you and are intuitive enough for anybody in the firm to access as needed. Backups of digital information are very critical, particularly when it comes to financial data. It is critical to keep them in a secure location to avoid potentially disruptive circumstances down the line.

Detailed Record Keeping

Proper bookkeeping allows you to understand the financial state of your company and what may become an issue in the future. It might be the difference between becoming a success story for a small business or not. At the same time, it can help to envision future forecasts and aid in company planning. "Know Your Numbers" is a statement Marcus Lemonis will repeat several times. First, of course, you must calculate how much money the company makes and how much it sells. And, while many entrepreneurs consider hiring an accountant to perform their taxes as needed, knowing your numbers entails much more.

For example, you should realize your firm's bank balances off the top of your head—at all times—how much your company is invoicing vs. how much you are spending, what your final production statistics were for last year, the gross and net profits of your previous quarter, and many other things. Therefore, it is critical to review your profit and loss statements (P&L) monthly, examine your general ledger, and comprehend all the figures you see. In addition, knowing how your company's accounts receivables and payables influence cash flow can allow you to make better decisions when needed rather than when it is too late.

You must make changes to your business every quarter to ensure that you stay on pace to meet your annual goals. It pays to clean up your records when it comes to excellent tax record keeping. According to the Internal Revenue Service, solid recordkeeping may accomplish much more. Here are three more ways that thorough records may benefit a small business owner.

Identify income sources: Using the books, you should distinguish between business and non-business revenues and taxable and nontaxable income.

Maintain a record of deductible expenses: everything should be noted as it happens to prevent leaving anything out when filing tax returns.

Support items stated on tax forms: If the IRS wants more explanation on the items reported on the tax returns, a comprehensive collection of precise and thorough documents will be important to speeding the investigation.

Keep Focus & Have Patience

To help you keep to a schedule and avoid distractions, make a "to-do list" every night before going to bed and start working on it first thing in the morning. However, it is critical to creating a realistic to-do list to avoid setting yourself up for failure. When beginning a new firm, it is critical to keep sight of a certain aim to assess success. You must first establish the overarching objective and then define smaller milestones that will progress you along the way. To help you keep to a schedule and avoid distractions, make a "to-do list" every night before going to bed and start working on it first thing in the morning. However, it is critical to creating a realistic to-do list to avoid setting yourself up for failure. That being said, it is equally critical to be resilient, not just in the face of everyday obstacles but also in the face of overall company outcomes expectations. Most successful firms do not emerge quickly; it may take years to reach their full potential and become a small business success story.

Be Prepared to Make Difficult Decisions

All business owners must make sacrifices for the sake of the company's success. However, there may come a time when the most difficult decision you must make is to set your ego aside. Pride may be fatal to a firm, and not all decisions will always reflect your values and ideals. And, while a small business owner should have significant personal and emotional stakes in the company, these should not be the driving force behind every daily decision. You should realize when you need assistance and understand that there are people who may know more about some elements of the business than you do. It is OK to seek assistance. You must be willing to leave your ego at the door and listen to what others have to say, especially if it comes from your consumer. It is difficult to approach a problem with humility and an open mind, but it is the only way to make smart business decisions.

Keep Your Overhead to a Minimum

"Cash is King," as the saying goes, and it is not incorrect; cash is one of the keys to small company success. Most business owners recognize the importance of capital liquidity as the first line of defense against any unanticipated problem. However, not all small firms can maintain a substantial enough reserve to sustain unexpected income losses or expenditure spikes. The bigger the cash flow, the more stable the organization; nevertheless, "50% of small enterprises operate with fewer than 15 cash buffer days" (JPMorgan Chase & Co., 2020.) One of the most crucial lessons that small companies learned from the coronavirus pandemic is how much cash it would need to pay overhead expenditures without an income? A reasonable rule of thumb is not to increase its overhead beyond what its cash reserves can support. It is far simpler to expand the firm as cash liquidity improves rather than being forced to reduce later because the business could not meet its overhead expenditures in an emergency.

Know the Operational Needs

You must understand everything about your company, and this knowledge should not be restricted to figures. It is critical to understand what the firm needs to function properly. Employees, equipment, supplies, and everything else required are all included. However, there is also the intangible component to consider. Efficient procedures and inventory management may have a significant impact on operating expenses. Researching best practices in a given sector and testing to see what works best for the firm (by trial & error) may be a time-consuming and laborious task. However, it will increase the profitability and performance of your company.

Hire the Right People and Treat Them Well

This is one of those areas that may come under making difficult decisions, but the firm must have A+ team players. All small business success stories have one thing in common: they understand that recruiting people is critical to their success. Every employee at a small firm, more than in a huge corporation, must be trusted to perform their daily tasks with as little monitoring as possible. To reduce overhead costs to a minimum, the structure must be as lean as feasible. As a result, no small firm can afford to squander a job by recruiting someone unsuitable for the position. The opposite situation, on the other hand, is true. A tiny firm cannot replace a stellar employee. Create a team and treat them properly. Pay attention to them and assist them in growing. The finest company executives build their teams because they understand that their teams will develop the firm. When it comes to hiring, it is critical to consider the sort of business culture you want to create in addition to expertise and skill. Candidates should be resourceful and capable of wearing several hats, especially at the start of the firm. When in doubt, choose the person who has all of the soft skills that are appropriate for the position and company culture, is trustworthy, and appears capable of learning the technical skills, rather than the one who simply excels at the technical skills and may cause problems with the team dynamic later. Your staff is the driving force behind the company. When it comes to selecting a new team member, attitude, charisma, and chemistry are crucial. "People who are more mentally healthy and happy tend to be better producers," says Tom Wright, Ph.D., a Kansas State University industrial-organizational psychologist and management professor who researches the impact of psychological well-being on work performance and employee retention. Employee happiness and well-being may greatly help the firm; the team typically performs more effectively when morale is strong.

Always Look to Improve

Avoid complacency and becoming oblivious to new ideas. When things start to go well and the company gets its stride, it's time to search for improved methods. Perhaps it is the automation of a manual component of the process, the addition of a new item, the creation of a distinct taste, or the opening of longer hours. Whatever it is, keep in mind that there is always the potential for development in every firm. To prevent getting stagnant, you must constantly move; innovation is required to make you a small company success story. Even companies with tremendous cash liquidity, such as Blockbuster Video, Kodak, and Borders Bookstore, suffered greatly due to their resistance to change. As soon as it becomes too comfortable, the rival will seize the initiative and find a method to overtake it. Consumer research can reveal pain areas that you were previously unaware of; perhaps a client's proposal will become the company's next success story. New methods to enhance your business will emerge organically if you are watchful, receptive, and listen to your staff and clients.

Chapter-05: How to Make Your Small Business More Successful

Focus on Customer Service

According to NewVoiceMedia research, 51% of customers will not do business with a firm again after a negative service experience. According to other research, it takes numerous positive client experiences to compensate for one unfavorable one.

Make exceptional customer service a priority since loyal consumers are much simpler to sell to. Examine your existing customer service and make the necessary modifications to guarantee that your small business provides superior service to your rivals. For example, you may need to engage in staff training, 42 6$tVBHYU9N8revamp your return policy, or make simple changes such as replying quickly to consumer voicemails or emails.

Build Word of Mouth for Your Business

Whether you run a business in a tiny town or a major city, word of mouth is more essential than ever. Most people use the internet to research business reviews before selecting where to purchase, thus developing a positive reputation is critical to your company's success.

How can you receive favorable feedback? Through delivering good, professional service, developing and monitoring your local (and internet) reputation, and earning exposure by supporting and sponsoring local groups and charities.

Expand Your Marketing Efforts

Effective marketing is critical to growing sales, but you don't have to spend a fortune advertising your company. There are several low-cost alternatives to promote your products and services, including:

- Making and utilizing a promotional kit
- Sending out promos in conjunction with your invoices
- Participating in professional groups
- Involve the media in your grand openings, relocations, or charity activities.
- Offering free courses or classes on your products or services
- Creating commercial alliances and cross-promotion with comparable enterprises
- Calling out of the blue (yes, it can still work)
- A car wrap is a great way to advertise your company on your vehicle.

Build Your Online Presence

Nowadays, creating a professional-looking website can be quick and easy, and your small business has to be online. According to an E-commerce Wiki study, 88 percent of buyers research goods online before purchasing in a shop. So for many small businesses, a simple website describing who you are, what you do, and how to reach you can suffice.

Testimonials from customers

Depending on your target audience, social media might be an excellent tool for promoting your company. Most companies today maintain a presence on social media sites such as Facebook, Twitter, and Instagram.

Cut Your Business Costs

Business expenditures for everything from office space to car expenses seem to be on the rise all the time, so keeping spending under control is a critical responsibility for business owners. However, keeping track of costs is time-consuming and tiresome, so use modern technologies wherever feasible to make the task as easy as possible. Various mobile apps for cost tracking are available, including several cloud-based accounting programs that allow you to automatically enter expense information into your accounting system by photographing receipts with your mobile smartphone.

Examine your key costs, like office space, business insurance, employees, and car expenses, on a yearly or semi-annual basis. Where can you shave? If you live in a location with plenty of available business space, you might want to consider relocating. On the other hand, you could start a home-based business if you don't require a storefront.

Examine your key supply prices regularly and seek discounts or methods to combine supply purchases with other firms to save money. Make cost-cutting a part of your job description and business culture.

Go Mobile

If you just accomplish one thing with mobile technology this year, make your online presence mobile-friendly, including your business website. People are increasingly using their phones to surf and search, even while they are at home. However, two other trends may be advantageous to your small business. The first of these is mobile marketing. You may employ several mobile-specific techniques to effectively reach your target demographic, ranging from text message advertising and mobile display ads to develop your company app.

Your second option is to use mobile payment methods. Apple Pay, Venmo, Square, Intuit GoPayment, Google Wallet, and Paypal are a few mobile payment options available. Offering pay-by-phone services is a huge convenience for clients, but your small business may save a lot of money using a mobile POS system.

Get in the Cloud

There is little doubt that cloud computing has leveled the playing field for startups, but the significant benefits of adopting the cloud for "regular" established firms are not usually emphasized.

The greatest benefits of transferring some of your company activities to the cloud are cost savings and access from anywhere. For example, suppose your company switches from a desktop small-business accounting program to a cloud-based accounting application. In that case, you will no longer need to install desktop software (saving IT costs for installation, backups, updates, and so on), and you will be able to access your business accounts from anywhere, including mobile devices. Of course, there are some drawbacks to cloud computing, but if you haven't begun utilizing cloud storage and applications yet, make 2018 the year that you do.

Find and Keep the Right Employees

One of the essential things you can do for your organization is attracting and retaining the appropriate workers. While recruiting and training people every other week may be the standard operating procedure for a fast-food restaurant, most successful businesses rely on employing excellent personnel and maintaining them long-term.

Update Your Business Plan

You did create a business plan before beginning your company, didn't you? A business plan is essential for new enterprises for various reasons, including determining the sustainability of your business concept and obtaining a loan or equity financing.

It's not too late if you haven't already created one. Successful, established firms revise their business plans annually to assess their successes (or lack thereof) and set new goals or directions.

The income statement, cash flow forecast, and balance sheet, which are included in the financial portion of the business plan, explain your company's financial health. From there, you may figure out how to make your company more lucrative by boosting sales, decreasing losses, or eliminating expenditures. If you want your firm to be more successful, you must devise a strategy for getting there.

Stay Balanced

Nobody goes to their grave wishing they had spent more time at work. But, unfortunately, to achieve their company objectives, too many business entrepreneurs compromise their mental and physical health, family connections, and friends.

Don't be one of them; instead, create a work-life balance that suits you. Getting enough sleep, spending time with family and friends, and exercising regularly will help you stay healthy and flourish in the long run.

Make This Your Best Year Ever

The main message is that success is not a guarantee. If you want your small business to succeed this year, you must make the necessary changes. That effort might be as easy as purchasing a new tool or as difficult as altering your mindset about certain company procedures. But you haven't gotten this far in your business only to let it stagnate, have you? So make the coming year your best yet.

Conclusion

Many websites will most likely tell you what to do when you start your small business, but they will not give you any advice or ideas to help your small business succeed. So, with that in mind, we've decided to share with our readers some of the top concepts you should implant in yourself to build the most successful small business. Of course, small company success does not happen immediately. To reach the intended outcome for your starting firm, you will need to be patient and persistent. However, the business growth and development ideas you use in your small business will only succeed if you apply them in the correct areas of your firm. So, first and foremost, conduct some studies within your company to identify places where you may use the concepts above.

Furthermore, continue to modify your business strategy as needed; only then will it work in your favor to make your small business the most successful. And, of course, you now understand what tactics and concepts you should employ to assist your small business in achieving its intended success. You will also learn from other small companies succeeding around you as you adopt these ideas and methods. Above all, you'll need to know how to put the strategies you've learned from other sources into action to convert your firm into a success. Finally, you should be aware that, in addition to implementing these creative ideas and methods, small companies require a dependable company management solution to help them on their way to success. A full company management system, such as WP ERP, maybe your single go-to friend on your path to small business success, making Human Resource, Customer Relationship, and Accounts management as simple as adding 2+2.

www.ingramcontent.com/pod-product-compliance
Lightning Source LLC
Chambersburg PA
CBHW030039230526
45472CB00002B/587